Color With Your Besties
Sherri Baldy
Coloring Books

About The Artist

Sherri Baldy is known for her trademark Big Eyed art for over 20 plus years around the world. She is a multi media artist that is licensed on a wide range of products. Sherri lives in Riverside, Calif. with her husband on their farm (Urban Farm Diva Farms) She has two sons Kyler & Josh & two daughter Courtney & Brittany.

When she is not painting, drawing and creating craft products for the craft industry, she spends her time in the gardens at the farm and in her "Barn Studio" that is open to the public by appointment.
Sherri Baldy is now offering her Big Eyed My-Bestie artwork in coloring books.
These fun coloring books come with 2 copies of each image for you to color, or better yet, have a Bestie party and color with one of your Besties Pals or keep them all to yourself :-)
Most of all have FUN, Color, Relax and Enjoy!

www.MyBestiesShop.com
Sherri Baldy My Besties Coloring Books in Riverside CA.
Copyright Sherri Baldy ~ My-Besties TM

Color With Your Besties
Sherri Baldy
Coloring Books

Welcome to My Besties World!

Sherri invites you to come join in her SUPER Friendly and FUN Crafting community!

We always look forward to seeing ALL the Sherri Baldy My-Besties Creations by our coloring, crafter friends from all around the world and We LOVE meeting and making NEW Friends!

Come PARTY with us every few weeks at our FB FUN NEW Releases where we have Loads of Giveaways, Name Games going on and Freebies!!!

We share tips, tricks and techniques. Join in on the FUN coloring & crafting group here:

https://www.facebook.com/groups/mybestiesdesigns/

Our crafty group is a safe fun place for you to post all your My Bestie Colorings, Creations, Photos, Blog Posts, and More..... anything featuring our My Besties Images, Stamps and Sherri Baldy Crafting Products are welcome!

We have MANY Shops for you to enjoy featuring Sherri Baldy My Bestie Craft Products!

Our My Bestie Shops:

www.MyBestiesShop.com

www.My-Besties.com

www.Scrapbookstampsociety.com

Our Etys Shop:

https://www.etsy.com/shop/SherriBaldy?ref=hdr_shop_menu

Join our Blog Challenges:

Our Sherri Baldy Blog:http://sherribaldy.blogspot.com/

Sherri Baldy

Color With Sherri & The Besties!

www.MyBestiesShop.com

Sherri Baldy My Besties Coloring Books in Riverside CA.

Made in the USA
Lexington, KY
03 April 2017